DOG

DOG

Joe Rosenblatt & Catherine Owen

Photos by Karen Moe

Mansfield Press

Printed in Canada

Library and Archives Canada Cataloguing in Publication

Owen, Catherine, 1971-
Dog / Catherine Owen and Joe Rosenblatt ; with photographs by Karen Moe.

Poems.
ISBN 978-1-894469-34-0

I. Rosenblatt, Joe, 1933- II. Moe, Karen III. Title.

PS8579.W43D63 2008 C811'.54 C2008-902404-4

Design: Mansfield Creative
Cover Images: Karen Moe
Edited by: Stuart Ross

Mansfield Press Inc.
25 Mansfield Avenue,
Toronto, Ontario, Canada M6J 2A9
www.mansfieldpress.net

The publication of *Dog* has been generously supported by the Canada Council for the Arts and the Ontario Arts Council.

Canada Council for the Arts | Conseil des Arts du Canada | ONTARIO ARTS COUNCIL CONSEIL DES ARTS DE L'ONTARIO

Dogs come to us from time to time ... as bearers of a special vision of the world. They are us — us as dogs ... perhaps the irony is that we are never more human than when we are dog.

Hélène Cixous

DOG

Gone to the Dogs

A Muse has no true master, it is said. Having begun by writing a baker's dozen of dog sonnets, in both conjoined and solo fashion, inspired by Karen Moe's photos of Cubano *perros*, we found ourselves incapable of resting on our doggy laurels. Suddenly the universe seemed to be exploding with canines of all persuasions, in the way that new parents find themselves prey on every street corner to a disgorging panoply of tots where prior they had scarcely taken mere juniors into account. The Dog chose to take us on a trip to the Milky Way and beyond, sussing out pups in constellations, lobbing mutts into the starry void and zinging them back into our imaginations, where they simmered in neuron light and the nubile romances of concocted mythopoesis. Kaboom! The heavens didn't hold us long, though, as more hounds pace the underworld than the firmament. Geez, Cerberus, how did ya string us on so long a leash? This multiple-mugged pup metamorphosed into a manifestation of seasonal affective disorder, the ghost of a freakish mother, and a birthing regurgitated. Dogs in nursery rhymes; Biblical mutts; pups set adrift on rafts in Istanbul; beatified dream fucking via osmotic doggy shape shifting; and best of all, old lovers and nemeses returning in houndish guise, wolves in memory's clothing, dripping with the scent of revenge. The Dog refused to muzzle us and so we willy-nillied in our fourteen-line kennels for months, content to gnaw on the rawhide of mystery, guarded by the benevolent psychopomp of cadence, imagination and mythical consciousness. The dog taking you to God knows where, as Lowell wrote in the grip of his own canine obsession. And now, as our universe sets into its wastrel intents, may your Dog be with you.

Joe Rosenblatt & Catherine Owen

Dog-Lobotomy (in doggerel)

Saddle-sore, hootenanied, kyboshed, my brain, from eighteen, on the junk of sombre,
found nodding in some Tin Pan alley of verse, cursed with rhythmic needles. They
dragged me in, the prose posse, straitjacketed my zip-zip,
threw this ditty in the clink, leg-ironed
enjambments. Nothin' doing. Those elegies kept
escaping, keening from my pen relentlessly.
So they strapped me in their hardcore de-worming machine, zapped
the skip from my nostalgia LP and gave me the cure
— a dog lobotomy.

Now my mind is on Fifi time, wired by schnauzers,
beagles, Great Danes, hell, I've even got a poodle
for a hypothalamus! No more lonesome lover tunes, my
Muse is all mutt and I'm loving it — unmuzzle me a sonnet,
will ya, how 'bout the fourteen-line dachshund ...

Catherine Owen

Drifting

I'm drifting like a piece of debris swept up by a leaf blower.
Sleep well, my fermentative rage, go and rest for an hour
and dream of a childhood's waltzing butterflies,
or perchance to follow the frothing pit bull in my soul:
Why wait? Get up, my faithful animal companion, Rex,
I need you to perform a creative ablution: it'll be beneficial
for us both, to lave and bless a grave via a bladder's ode
to a slippered ghost, hunched over like a dead plant.
In the citreous light I see her sporting a treacled smile
as she shuffles about some dirt floor in a worm-starred abode.
Yes, my grinning friend, you and I can co-scribe a poem,
but I am out-surged by your stream of consciousness.
You write so effortlessly and are so damned elegiac!
You didn't learn the craft in some puppy mill, did you?

Joe Rosenblatt

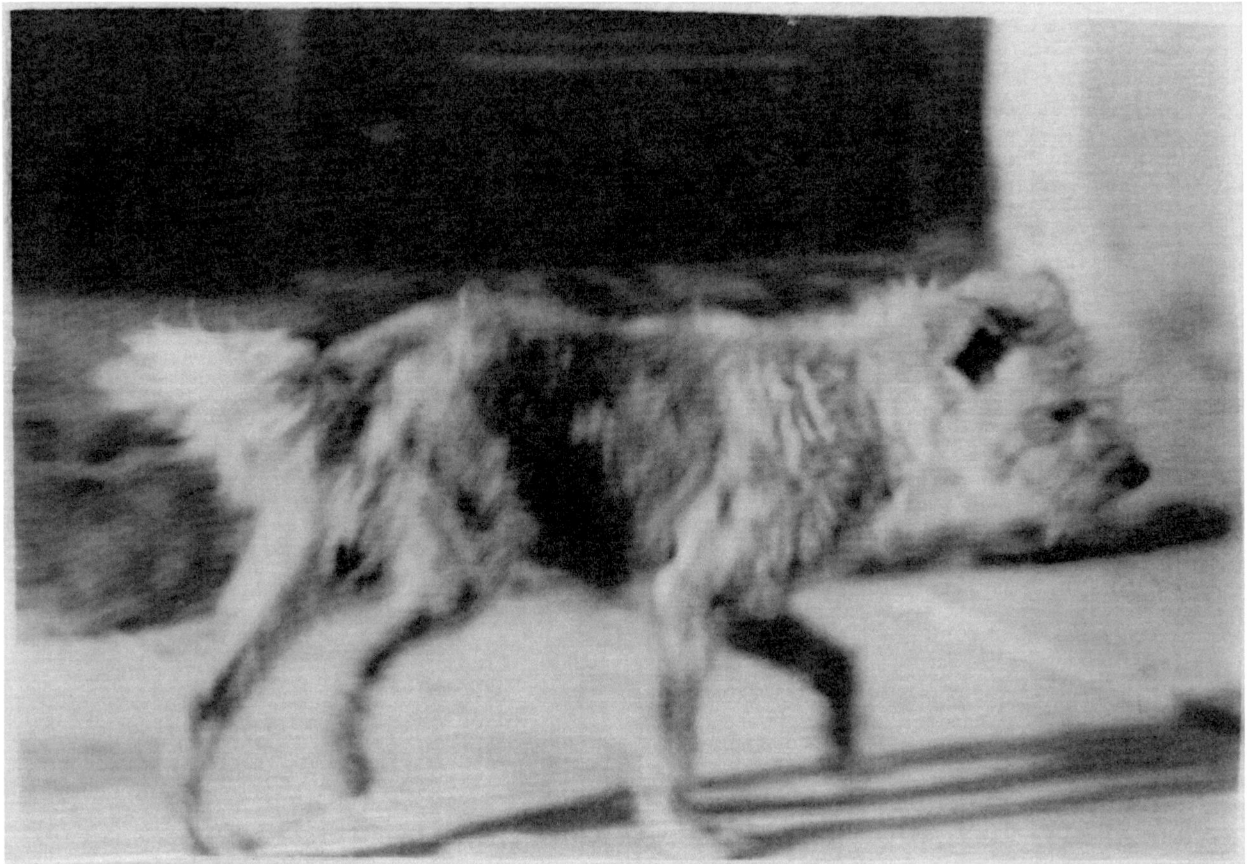

Roam

Shaking fleas off its ghostly coat
my flagging spirit trails behind
the body roaming down a road.
I've seen that dog who herds my sleep
although he will not fetch my slippers.
Keep moving, soul, but not too fast, and not too slow.
Where are you going — where's the fire, are you alive
or are you dead — yet does it matter in the bite of life?

The road wells in my eye like a tear.
So many acres fathomed; so many lost.
Who calls this dog that lures my dreams into pens,
pastures, manifold enclosures? He will
not fetch a stick, neither will he beg, yet life's bite
stirs his paws to rambling; my spirit follows.

Joe Rosenblatt & Catherine Owen

Canis Major, Big Dog

Our Big Dog, a happy spectre, is fast asleep
while gaseous fireflies attack his floppy ears.
Only God, his trainer, can hold his sparkly leash
that's tethered to a sizzling necklace of Eternity:
I view his phosphorescent tongue and eyes:
they're combustive fields that radiate intelligence.
Do you think our Master would handle a stupid pet?
This Dog herds hulking bears around the sky!

A mighty herder is our working Dog, and bless his pups!
Have we met before — were you employed in a scrapyard
of some inner city? You who are the pit bulls of my faith
eat well, dine heartily, you must ingurgitate the race
so gnaw the flesh clean off the shank of longevity.
Look star-ward, friend, don't you see those frightened bears
racing toward a dark abyss that is the stomach of the night.

Joe Rosenblatt

Chicken Bone

In the final analysis aren't we all chicken bones?
Why deny the tail and mouth of a pure gastric principle?
Take me, for instance, am I not a pattern — my own bone tree
for a gnawing canine of fate honing his pointy incisors?
An adorable dog has picked me out of a garbage bin:
I am now mere history, nothing more than an obscene comedy.
The darkness throws up its meal only to swallow an octet —
this ravenous wanderer is on a sacred mission.

Unlike Aesop's dog with his steak, no mere
reflection will provoke my plangent yapping; I gaze
down into the well of the world from this thin bridge
and ask not for another chicken bone — one
limb is victory enough — its pale moth of food quivers,
caught in the dwindling light of my mouth.

Joe Rosenblatt & Catherine Owen

The Beggar

I saw a dog step out of the ash.
It was no one I recognized; it wasn't
the wet eyes of my childhood, those spree
ears I loved sprung out of a window as the car
(liquid in a freeway breeze) shot past all my landscapes.
The ash clung to its fur in tiny black stars; the scent
of *Blue Moon* sung by small Catholic campers
clung to its fur. It was not my grandmother;

it was no one I recognized; it was not Frank,
reeled back from absence; it was not Mark
in his sailboat, *The Iliad*. The ash grew a spark
like that emptied fire in the mind and the dog
did not weep like Jesus but on his haunches
sat in the cooling, anonymous and meek.

Catherine Owen

Pounce

If you touch me you'll feel a surge of rage.
I have this urge to taste your blood, drive
my teeth into the shank of your ogling pity.
You *turistas* shall have no dominion over me.
I'm not your common street waif, I'm housed in pride!
My immaculate ears are the antennae of piety
for when the sun sets I'll bay at my master illumed
inside a burning bush on some sidewalk in Havana.

Ignore my Tudor hide, gristle lines my shadow, Che's
fierce love has sprung my posture. Not even *perros*
escape the virility of the imagination: I'm Cagney,
I'm Brando, I'm Capone! The heat swells my eyeballs
to fruit ripened in alleyways; I crouch over your grave,
turista, the one the camera carves in your mind.

Joe Rosenblatt & Catherine Owen

Slut

You trollop of the cobblestones, tongue
slurped up in a lick on life's cone, Havana
back alleys, your bordello — what are you seeking?
Hair once *frou-froued* in a white fluff coiffure,
eyes pepped with the hot sights of scraps, now
your coat mats, ears sag and pudenda pulses,
an overstuffed sac above the pavement ...
the small olives of your eyes dull.

Famished angel, the evening is your mother.
She will place you gently on her lap, calm you
and cover you snuggly under a tattered blanket.
A portly moon will be your only friend.
Your breath spirals up to a starry landing —
there you'll find a frowzy rug on the floor:
Darling, slip into something comfortable.
Rest your head against the pillow of the night.

Joe Rosenblatt & Catherine Owen

Homo Homini Lupus

Man is a wolf to man is what I am in my pelt.
In me howls the beast and yet there's no moonlight
to brighten my cave of venomous reminiscence; nurtured
by a three-headed howler I drank her bilious lactose;
this, too, I've repressed; but still the memory throbs
like phosphorescence swimming inside an aperture
that leads into some wormhole of a stellar-studded stomach
wherein I know my true biological mother dwells
jellied in ether, her quavering voice calling out to me
in a recurring dream, and me cringing like a dark pup
whimpering under the ectoplasmic security blanket
of my mongrel soul; curse her matrix, all that DNA
that formed her birth canal, and yours truly spawned forth,
writhing, gurgling, a whelp snipped free from the cord, a disease!

Joe Rosenblatt

A Hound Called Cerberus

What a dysfunctional family confronted our Cerberus!
Imagine him an unhappy pup tearing at the flesh of the dead
as they descend into Hades, ripping and rending with scarcely blood
to slurp; it must have warped all his fifty heads, a multiple
personality disorder; consider his mum, she, part serpent, part woman,
and his dad — a fire-belching control freak covered
in a dermal embossment of snakes and dragons, ah, in stark human contrast
psoriasis is but a zit on the very tip of a teen's beak!
My favourite pit bull of a psyche, is he not the perfect guardian
of some biker's scrap metal yard. Visualize the sign stopping trespassers:
Warning: Rex awaits you past these gates — or possibly the sign
isn't there at all, although shards of flesh and bone fragments litter the yard.

Dear Mom: I never did send you my letter telling you about my new job,
asking you to come and visit and bring some overcooked chicken.

Joe Rosenblatt

Dolorous Dog

Dolorous dog, moon dog, and mother dog
frostier than a pit bull, but less loyal.

May the dogs of Eternity gnaw on her bones. Mother, kiss thy
fundament in the ghost world;

Your loving dog son eats his chow, sorts out his kibbles,
regurgitates, and pukes: should

a grateful dog son honour his ingrown mother? Or should he chew
upon his Master's Commandments,

sharpening his incisors, doggedly toughening his grit, honing his
loathing in the jaws of integrity.

With no light in her reptilian eyes, she dimly asks: "Can you buy
a *mudder* in Eaton's ... ?"

I think of a calcified pup found in its mother's womb
and I dwell on Cerberus pissing on the gates of hell.

Joe Rosenblatt

Red Dog

Prone to scatological outbursts, and an obsessive
doggedness to advocate familial cleansing: yes,
if only my thoughts were serrated and the dead
could be resurrected to extend their necks
to an obedient son; but then incisors could rend
any nonagenarian's wattled throat on a sunny day.
Dare I go into oscillation, plead poëtic license, visions
embellished with jerks and grimaces like a mutt
crinkled with fleas, swarming and feeding
on a Tourette's pelt of succulent matricide — I'm a red dog
with three nattering minds: wanting to pee on a hydrant,
on a bad poem written by a poet laureate, or perchance to dream
of watering a mother's grave: *Sleep well, you're in a nebulous kennel*
ogled by twinkling dog catchers.

Joe Rosenblatt

Hey, Medusa Momma

Hey, Medusa momma, I see you got some dancing curls!
Hey, momma, what's that wriggling on your snowy head?
Hey, momma, marbled in memory — you got me stoned on hate.
Hey, momma, how's your budgie doing in the spirit world?
Hey, slippered momma, shuffling about like an old arthritic dog.
Hey, momma, get a sniff of me; I'm not getting old, merely decomposing!
Hey, momma, your latkes have freezer burn; but then I'm a hungry schnauzer of a son.
Hey, momma, *"Can I buy a mudder like you in the bargain basement of Eternity?"*

Hey, Medusa momma, love those hissing ringlets on your prehistoric pate!
Hey, momma, a tinted photo, circa 1920 — is that you in a butchy sailor's outfit?
Hey, momma, you always wore the pants, and papa wore a short leash.
Hey, momma, your pacemaker — has the warranty finally run out?
Hey, momma, fruit flies hover around the rubber plants — turn down the heat!
Hey, momma, are you dead, and renting out your ghost kennel in Hell?

Joe Rosenblatt

The Dog-Children

If the womb is a living kennel, then my whelps
gnawed clean through its walls, their caul
the Croat flag, rent by superstition's fleas.
When sixteen teats did not sate, they clawed
all my flesh into nipples and tossed me hard
on my side — a mother-shank from Maternity's Butchers.
Slippers were spent to confetti, an acid-rag left for carpet,
drapes worried to cud and blood yelping everywhere.

There was nothing in my heart they left pure
and yet I did not tie them in a river-bound sac, did not
slit them silent at the jugular, and dreaming of their deaths
made me weep, ravaged as Hecuba who, in the finality of loss,
could only bark like a dog the mad bond — the mad bond! —
its dark leashing and releasing her.

Catherine Owen

Happy Perro

A breeze unseals the day's thick heat.
Streets peel off their rancorous transactions, spill
fervent siestas into the boulevards, dogs
and people frolicking in Fahrenheit's plummet,
the tails of their minds twirling unfurled. "Released,
released!" they squeal beyond doors. His body
a lick of the darkest lightning, dancing
inside Havana's hunt for escapades.

He rumbas on streets where contented spirits converge,
where succulence of mind hangs like meat upon a T-bone
and a smiling canine can meet the bourgeoisie in heaven.
Karen, can it be your Happy *Perro* is happier than me
though you should never feed a dog in love a chicken bone.
Life splinters like fragile cartilage; all is illusion, except meat,
more meat, an oven-fresh baguette, good red wine and gorgonzola.

Joe Rosenblatt & Catherine Owen

Tonton: The Dog That Was Enclosed in an Acorn

Flibbertigibbet! Plipped out, nubbin-headed, ladled
scoop of hound, morsel-poppet, miracle-mutt dubbed
by the latest Make-a-Stink Foundation, *National Enquirer*
stray amid alien potentates, I Kissed Satan twaddle, ELVIS sightings —
what mad tree did you fall from? Was your *madre*
the May Queen or, like Ariel pincered in the cloven pine,
did you run afoul of your own rank Sycorax?

I imagine a chamois-lined womb,
and in the amniotic sap, a damp pup,
pawing. If the three-week-old fetus
is a moth, then you will peck out, tail
first, a dog-tuber, and will not fear
the earth's dark, nosing up your own
tough bark, unburying bones.

Catherine Owen

Apocalypse Dog in God's Starry Pantry

Lobbed up into the heavens by the force
of an ignited hemisphere, my claws
scritch on the firmament, God's Sistine kitchen

spattered with a bouillabaisse of comets, petit-
four stars, pots and pans swimming with milky
constellations. Eternally unleashed, I
pad my vast domain on fine unfettered
legs and yip beyond the muzzle

hosannas of ecstasy — *"Quel consommé! Buenos nachos!"*
No kibbles malinger in dry bowls. No water
toils with gnats — I'm the fattest dog star
in the sky, gobbling Orion's picnic, indifferent
to Earth's crumbling biscuit where commands
once fed me — belching a jig on the farthest planet from the sun.

Catherine Owen

Loyalty

Betcha wish there was a dog-utopia somewhere, like
Burroughs' boy-island, say, a land of canine companions,
ever eager to fetch sticks, slippers, newspapers, but with free
& wild intent, to trot alongside you over the frangipanied moors,
to muff around your feet before night's fires. Dogs are humans
without the guile, without those neat checkmarks of lust.
Icarios, crying murder, was sought by his pup, Maera,
who dragged her master's body to justice
under the rising light of Procyon while

Xanthippus's dog swam to Salamis from Athens after the hull
of his exiled ship. Even if dogs are forgotten, they retain
a seed of their beloved's face. Argos was the true Penelope.
He died of joy at his lost king's return while
Telemachus chose interrogation over embrace.

Catherine Owen

A Dog's Concordance to the Holy Book

Hey, Fido! You're no Fifi in the Bible, you know, no
coddled, fondled *chien* of leisure, chucked under the chin
by Abraham, scratched behind the ear by Moses.
Fidelity? Love? Watchful care? It's not until the medievalists
that such epithets swarm you with the joy of a flea's festival.
Here you: drag, prowl, snarl, surround, devour, lick
blood from stigmata, but, mostly, eat.
Greatest Old Testament threat? May your corpse
be thrown to the dogs! Scarcely a man's best friend, those
mutts from Babylon, Jezebels of table scraps!
Old English lore tells of St. Christopher, JC's
hardy ferryman, having the head of a hound, but

the scholars must have buried this vision, a bone
in sleep's pitted, vast precinct.

Catherine Owen

Dickinson's Dog

Great lumbering pup Carlo, named far
From the ice house in Amhurst, Newfie
Burnt with the fervency of Jane Eyre,
Missionary bark in the Valentine's Day fur
Of a suitor lost deep in Miss Emily's small,
Twine-sewn bundles. Long before she wore
White and fled at the Butcher Boy's step,
The dog, its hills and sundown were the trinity

She converted to. Carlo was a Puritan, a good
Excuse for aloofness, his shaggy ears easily offended
By the *unhallowed things people speak of*, he, a sacred
Guardian of her innermost dashes, warm and Mute *Confederate*,
Miss Emily, at his death, asking Higginson for instruction,
Now that this one sure bit of sky had gone out of her life.

Catherine Owen

Carne No Pan

Little spurn of the lens, little twitch, tail
a whip of furred licorice, unfinished
question mark, you leave on cat feet
like the fog. The street bleats out its dream
in tunnel-white and trip-trop, your infinitely tiny
nails, innocent of fate, scritch on the vanquished
cobblestones. A sifted light wavers; who
from the darkness comes? Hosts of cages

line history's ambivalence, at each one *Turista*
hovers with a stick, only wanting
(wholly innocent) each beast in its ark or if not ark
then dinner (this is the law — dog eat dog — remember?).
But then too it was never the Lion of God
who took away the sins of the world.

Catherine Owen

A Ghost Dog in Love

Purpled in silk, and reclined on an organdy couch
you stirred in your dream to the touch of this beast
painting your lean oiled thighs with a spirited tongue.
"I'm all furry inside," he cried. His brazen paws knew
the terrain, as though they'd been there before: a fragrance
climbed to his nostrils, and then awakened his large grey eyes.
"Is this some bouquet for a ghost dog in love?" he moaned.
"It's the apple-scented breath of my soul," came your reply.
"I must have it," he growled, and pressed his wet long snout
to her throat, finally coming to rest, asleep at her breasts.
Fate wears an amorous collar tethered to a platinum leash;
yet they who resist Lechery's adorable perfume have no pulse
or breath, but exist as phantoms padding stealthily into a bog;
whining and barking they sink into the briny muck of Eternity.

Joe Rosenblatt

Phantom Dog

I'm your salivating beast, a phantom dog.
From my invisible world I move toward you
stealthily like a silvery moth under a starless sky.
Shivering, you've become my sparkling eyes;
my large paws weigh heavily on your thighs
brailing your body, trust me, I'm your guide dog;
follow my footsteps away from the darkness.
Metamorphosed as sunlight, let us enter my lair.

Gristle, shards of bone, and the soul, too, consumed
with its platinum feathers, truly an iridescent meal;
for love is the tiniest of briskets, and hardest to view,
mangle and chew, and absorb in lechery's saliva.

Let us ingurgitate our reckless moments together.
My paw rests on your heart; I give you my breath.

Joe Rosenblatt

EL FLECHA
BESOS

Besos

"If this be my twelfth labour..." and here
Heracles, in light's last pang, paused,
for the dog in his mind furled black lips
back over racks of thrice-bared teeth, a hundred eyes
spawning from six, staring him thin as a sizzle
of rain on the noon-high plaza. Kafka's
machine inscribed the sins of language; flesh
amending its transgressions — "Turn over,

Doppelgänger, you're not done yet!" Who
loves a Cerberus indeed, door to the underworld
when all one wants is sleep? Heracles
severed the heads but a shadow always returns
on its platter, shining behind walls hewn with exile's
utterings, to snarl, "Kiss me, you sword-drawn fool!"

Catherine Owen

Chara Crashes My Party

Wanting to meet the neighbours in my beaming galaxy
I threw a block party, offered misty refreshments:
silvery martinis, sparkling highballs, transgendered
cyanide shooters, methane chasers and other volatile potations;
things were humming along, revellers stoned in orbit on Krypton
and then Chara has to crash my party, enflaming my guests.
She's all over me, wants to swamp the black abyss of my heart
with drool, put her itch on my nerves; she's such a gas,
always cruising for expectorating sex with a stranger.

"Get your jigging pup off my jewels," squeals a burning ember.
"She's turning me into a soupy mire of my former self!"

The paws of my muse are upon me: her eye incandescent.
You'd think she owned all the glow in the vault of heaven —

Come on, baby, light my hydrogen with your puppy eyes!

Joe Rosenblatt

Snow Dog

December's Easter, this resurrection of white
when his nose, a white crocus, snubs
above the bank, softest apparition.
Incandescent dog! No fleck of spring
on his pelt, but stoical forms, Nordic
stringencies, a bark that won't melt
in our long night's fear. Embayed
by his bulk, we are saved; the snow

protects its own cold denizens, makes
of ice a messiah. I am your snow dog,
my paws extend toward Absence.
Wearing a winter collar, unleashed,
a raving wind howling my name; memory,
can I retrieve you, out where I've never been?

Joe Rosenblatt & Catherine Owen

Childhood Dogs

for Keppoch

Dogs are the politics of neighbours.
Mounting my fleet Marmaduke, I knew this: Rusty, the rag-mutt
with a nose like a soft fist, put to sleep after he thieved one of my dolls, stabbed tooth
marks in the plastic quim. Or the terriers next door who keeled my sister into fear —
nights she would scream awake, dreams of saucer-eyed fiends, pups with eyes parsed as
mill wheels. Grief is never far from dogs:
Mrs. Hanson's slippered cries when her Darling Cocoa clipped a car; Mr. Morgan
faltering after his blind pug woke cold; Toro keening in the pear tree for his absent
master. They're the renegade thread in the suburbs: Kelly, lawn-shitter;

Spooks, garden-router; Paris, devourer of aperitifs. The Dogs of Istanbul, bucking reform
on all three legs, were shipped out on a steamer, like the Fools of Kreuznach,
their primitive element too relentless for the new regime. There is no tame
in a dog, but that bought hard by humans, at the price of a Cerberus snarling
at the bright gates of Hell, keeping depths.

Catherine Owen

Siamese Dogs

Wearing titanium suits fused at the navel,
shadows merging in the lunar light.
Two dogs by the Sea of Tranquility,
we're glued umbilically to one mind.

We share a few heart valves, and yet
the blood between us reaches no isthmus
but courses like stars seen by the macula lutea,
that sensitive fraction of the eye's witness.

An opalescence pulsates in a smoky theatre:
moving softly on sooty wings, flecks of night
take flight, flutter around this blazing corona.

We'll not settle for an effigy's stasis ... our barks ululate
across galactic distances to other moons; no pale icons
these molecular fantasies orbiting beyond the flesh.

Joe Rosenblatt & Catherine Owen

I'm in Your Dream

I'm in your dream, curled up on your bed
at your feet, and do you feel my hard wet snout
moving up where it shouldn't, nuzzling gently ...
Surrender — useless to resist these heavy paws
dominant, weighing on your small shoulders.
We are together now, lie still, don't be afraid,
the animal night won't bite you, my grin, notice
its toothy luminescence, and a firm tongue pressed
at your throat, don't worry: I'm a friend;
run your fingers through my coat, embrace me,
a hunched grey shadow, let me be your pillow.
Put your head back, enjoy this undulating dream:
but enough of this billowy pillow talk. *Yes, I am bad.*
Stare directly into my lunar eyes, searching you.

Joe Rosenblatt

Carne

A white shadow with a narrow tapered face.
Barely visible, you're a fading dog of history,
wearing a tight little smile, a stigmata on your brow,
eyes bright as fiery zircons, meatless beast.
Carne, I could be you shining in the noonday heat.
Posing for the camera you wear my conscience
like a splayed tail tied to a battered tin can.
Comedian of the underworld, be my companion.
Enter the doghouse of my soul, and stay awhile.
Mock me with your laughing tongue, and add
a lick of cobalt to the palette of my melancholia.
Miserable wraith, gnaw upon my personality,
rip and tear, here and there, cleanly off the bone!

Shape shifter, we've met before in some puppy mill.

Joe Rosenblatt

Dog, Disappearing

As in Goya's quicksand, that turbulent
marble of land, vortex and innocent, your head,
plumb with history, a lumpen mass
bobbing above death — ears
pricked for anythinganything,
nose a dark, damp bubble —

the mud clogs your collar, jewelled
with dog tags, their shim battered
by a brown scumble of hues, a Gadarene universe,
pocked with Napoleon's cannons.

Yet perhaps you know your sleep
will be short, a light curl inside loss —
your eyes still lit between canthi,
life wagging.

Catherine Owen

My Darkness

Those aren't my crazy mother's scornful eyes
enveloping me in drowning pools of adoration,
for in the lunar light devouring my stony gaze
I see some dark stranger enter a sparkly spa.
Her glowing face seems disquietingly familiar.
Did we once embrace and couple by candlelight?
But was it me that flickered, or was it that candle?

It was in my last troubled incarnation
I saw her try to escape from a gothic painting
while a misty emanation filled our haunted bedroom
spiralling down the staircase of a winding mansion.

Newly mineralized and vulnerable, my soul
spins giddily around this orbicular lady:
Love's gravitational pull has dragged me into orbit.

My Bleeding Heart, go and fetch my darkness!

Joe Rosenblatt

Moon Dog

In the dim night of the mind's wilding rack, I walk
beneath another creatured moon, its frozen orb
entrained to pounce upon those thoughts that crawl
my tongue's red plank. I'm your howling Anubis.
I direct the carrion traffic: I'm your raving guide,
your substitute companion in some altered guise,
inevitable hyena, embalmer's friend, or One
who leads the Blind into an incorruptible world.

Tragic animal! If I dog you, it's to see you through the Dark —
You're less than Argus-eyed; if stones be the mouth of grief,
then you've blunted my rainbows, bruised my light's vast milk.
Darling, I've got the coins; let's meet our Boatman.
We must cross that fetid river this evening.

Must you put on a puppy face when you yowl?

Joe Rosenblatt & Catherine Owen

Gloom-Mutt

So it's you again with your paws of mud, fuddy-duddy
of depression. At Terminus Station, the hellhounds
unchained your dog cart, and, dullard-pup, you derailed
into my cortex, snuffling. No lewd Actaeon
mauled by slavering fiends; no Sin disembowelled
by a canine corset; you're pathetic, a slumping,
runny basset, chunnering Chow-Chow, poodle
of youth's last howl; and I not even your master.

You frothing beast, come share my tomb of light.
Let's coalesce in mystic glue and tame our urges,
but leave conjoining to sonneteers and fools.
My melancholic stray, join me in the sunroom
where triple-headed monsters bark and snuffle
while doing a grind at their Gloom Mutt Cabaret.

Joe Rosenblatt & Catherine Owen

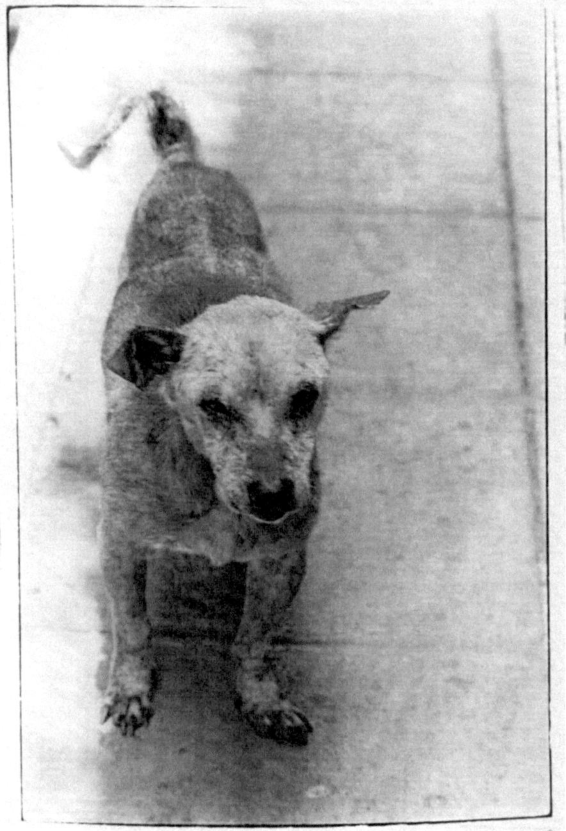

Scrappy

Life carries a machete through an acre of hell.

We dig into ourselves to discover a solitude
found on a bone scraped clean by some honing knife.
We remain invisible, loving this comforting silence.
What a strange archaeological site we've become!
We're shaped like some dog yet know we're human.
Perhaps we've come to the end of an alleyway
where glazed aromas assault us from a kitchen:
a ghostly snout strides ahead of a waxing face,
turns about and drools in celebration of our escape.
"Someone light a match," screams a serrated voice.
"I can't feel my body — a starving dog has eaten it!"

Joe Rosenblatt

Cynocephalus: The Song of a Dog-Headed Man

Hey, baby, shine your eyes on me, 'cause a dog-headed man
just makes the best loving man, so feed me kibbles and bits,
some honeyed kisses, some wiggles and snuggles too, do
what dogs do carelessly, love is a meal, let's get personal!
Hey, baby, don't be scared, I won't bite your fluttery hand.
I just want your pale green sculptured nails to nibble with gusto
and don't put a studded diamond collar around my hairy neck
I'm not some common mutt you get from the local pound.
Let lust, romance and dirty pillow talk warm us up in bed
dirty as my shaggy body rollin' in the mud. O baby,
this dog's going to do you good — he's canine-crazy-for-you
wagging. No, don't be frightened of my tapered lovin' snout
'cause the dog-headed man, he's a woman's best friend
so chill and groove awhile on my tongue made of silk.

Cynocephalus 2: The Lady's Reply to the Dog-Headed Man

Dearest dog-headed man, I hate to use slang but you sound
sluttish as one of those Lickasaurus hounds, a gross
hirsute mutt, a Rover's-got-his-bone, just lookin' to paw my panties
down, hunting honey with your hyperbolic puppy lust.
Who do you think I am? One of your unwashed women bitches
with her tail between her haunches and hair like Brillo pads?
Your serenade may enchant them but to me it sounds like wolves
gone mad so get back to your sheep-suckling pasture and stop
hangin' round my nectar or I'll tell you what I'll do!
I'll wrench your elongated snout, twist it to an oblong isle,
expand your nostrils, yank your pointy ears, now listen —
don't tell me your paw moved by kinesis, next you'll be
yappin' that this raunchy woman-handling paddle is your daddy's ghost.
I'll decapitate you, hound, hang your head on my trophy wall!

Joe Rosenblatt & Catherine Owen

Ex-Dogs

I.

Three million gallons of urine! 1000 tons of excrement!
A day's doggy tally on Britain's Shakespearean streets — and you,
William the Wastle's abject pup, poncy of a castle crapped
by underlings. He's got you on his leash — you can't fool me —
bit of a clothesline his Mam doesn't miss, collarless and rucked
with fleas, ticks in the ear, worms up the bum — a dumb lot, this dating
service, pairing mutt & master with a dirty quotient, a dim-witted meter.
Dogs are tough to shame — witness the fuck-locked puppies on a street
in Bogotá, pelted by rocks, razzed and still merrily at it, unstoppable.

Like you, bulldog pomp in a dachshund's posture, memory-can
scavenger, muscling up to the reddest hydrant to find it drenched
with Eau-de-Rover, your feeble drizzle changing nothing
as the reflections of countless bones
float past in your rivals' streams.

2.

Old Blue Bell, you ne'er-do-well pup, celler-gadder, quim-sniffer, your
chin's mucked with coal scuttles. Sent to fetch a thousand times, no stick's
in your maw but your matted fur's cleft with dogbane. You're the mutt
scurrying back to the Bible though it spat you out of Eden, scraping
together a kennel from scraps of women's kindness.
Playing dead soon loses its charm, shake a paw peters out even
in the realm of doggerel, but look — she's left behind some rawhide!
Chomp on that, mongrel-mouth! Original stray hound of Mandelstam's den,
now a shotgunned carcass in your past's gulag. But wait! Once,

you were a Rottweiler of sorts, pugnacious pug, in their faces, on their
legs, humping fishnet, twill, an unmuzzled will lunging at meaty intruders.
Now your bark is as worn as your incisors. Fat, you piddle on the mat
by the fire, chase dodos in your arthritic sleep and worry not, for your
Sweet Lady is sure to stuff you when you croak — a faithless dog's last dream.

Catherine Owen

A Pit-Bull's Revenge

A rodent called Charles was wisping along the lean lawn of life
scavenging for scabs to add to his farrago of wounds
when I spied him, stabbing a deep hunger in the viscera,
my maw growling for revenge — the smell of memory
offended me — as if it was an old piece of cheese.
It was this very rat, I tell you, who gobbled scraps
from the bowls laid out to feed my pups, whose tail whipped us
with a dominatrix lust, whose beady eyes and rank scruff
popped up above every chance to quit the puppy-mill, squeaking —
"not yet my foppish mutt — I haven't yet milked your every kindness!"

I slavered at this ambush of the past, becoming rabid
that this ingrate rat still lived. Busting off my muzzle
with a satanic yowl, I pounced, and that finking rodent,
that slithering gray gobstopper of life, didn't know what hit him.
Before he could squirm free, I had his knackers between my teeth,
shaking him like a rat-maraca while giving him the pit-bull glare.
Charles, after all his bravado, was scared; his corpse, though thin,
made a fine rug for the pups and I to dream on.

Catherine Owen

The Pickup

"So what's a cat person like you doing in a dog
sonnet like this?" Chuck asked, his ratty teeth
flashing as he sashayed up to the bar, tail a-droop
as his cadence. Deign to answer him? I did, but with
hidden motivation. "See, Monsieur Gris, cats are like
wives, familiar in a mysterious sort of way, sloe-eyed,
deliciously whiskered with pelts of melting purrs
and whistled play, wholly copious and disdainful,
sullen or coy as the moment finds them, but mine
to fry the fish for. Dogs are Muses."

Chuck seemed confused, scritching his withered head
at such distinctions. "But" — I continued — "they have *one* similarity
between them." "Yes?" — he struck a pose,
listening. "They both love rats for din-dins ... " And
before that bristled runt could flee, I grabbed his rump, you
snatched his neck, and, for once, Chuck made nary a squeak.

Catherine Owen

Footprints

Footprints face me down a laneway.
It looks like I'm going in circles, although
I belong to someone, please note my plebian collar
and short leash; I'm staring up at you, but don't try
enticing me with your charm: what are you hiding
in your knapsack? I smell ripened waftings from heaven!
Do you have something for Mr. Personality? I'm subbing
for the Gotham Joker, my titanium white side
surrounded by lunar darkness. You're a dream
I've been waiting for all my life, I feel
this surge of eyeball-to-eyeball veracity ...
I'm wearing a saucy grin, flashing a jovial feed-me tongue.
Take my picture, go ahead, capture my alpha soul — I'm ready —
Thieve my heart, though next time, wear a love belt of wieners!

Joe Rosenblatt

A Heavy Paw

"Follow your footprints," a voice cried out,
and like a homeless dog my soul wandered,
inhaling decay down an alleyway of the night
until it met a dog with flashing teeth.

"Do I know you?" I said, meeting his gaze.
"The trail ends here," the Dark One replied.
"You've come a long way, now lie down and rest."

Like coral burning at the bottom of an angry reef
a wavering light escaped from his mouth.
And his eyes incandesced

as though they were set on some invisible string
worn by a famished demon happily wagging his tail
while raising a heavy paw to claim
a flank of meat from a camera-wielding tourist.

Joe Rosenblatt

Sun Dog

To a crystal of diffracted ice
illuming a body beautiful, my spirit,
a dancing sun dog in the sky, conjoins
pulsing with another glowing lover.
My burnished pup, you have relinquished
the voiceless dark to yowl these rays
which shape a reliquary of our night
consigning my grief to a glint beyond auroras.
Deep within a ghost cocoon where souls pupate
and hum inside some twinkling kennel
vibrating their canticles to other stellar pups,
I caress your luminous pelt and yearn
for martyred Sebastian arrowed on earth,
his heart haloing the darkness.

Joe Rosenblatt & Catherine Owen

Black Dog

I'm all aglow in delicious despair.
I have more guilt on my body
than Cerberus's mom had teats.
Born inside his drooling jaws,
I was shared among his famished heads
who devoured me at the Gates of Hell,
and finding me unappetizing they vomited.
As a corrosive stream I flew out of three mouths!

But worse was yet to follow — this Gorgon had mates:
Geryon's gang of two, Orthos & Gargittos, Hades'
quattro-tongued street cleaners!
I, a crucifixion of puddles, those lapping dog-flaps drawing nearer,
and Heracles dead as God, shrunk from doom with all the lavish force
of the flames that Dixie in my self's caustic sea.

Joe Rosenblatt & Catherine Owen

Street Dog

for Matthew

She was the black shape your innocence took — how
long on the streets — this Hades of half-cut, take-out, dead-
end days squatting by the Figmart with thin, insistent
arias — *Can you spare some change*? She sat firm
at your feet — a figurehead on the street's Ship of Fools
or snailed around your cup on the rag, drab
square of a blanket.

A dog dreams your final Ararat, the olived
land you still someway long for at the clink
of each coin's sound, hum of junk's burnt veins, cold's
jolt through the spine like Hydra. I saw her once —
lapping the apertures of your wounds, she doctor at it and gentle,
or another time I watched you dance with her, girlish
and tender — her tail knowing Elvis, assuagement, the pariah night.

Catherine Owen

The Dogs Of Istanbul

Packs I read of in Flaubert, prowling
Taksim Square, lurching along the Bosphorus,
spotted, gruff, randy as the pong of fish,
wild herds zipping through wheels of carriages,
hearses, kebaps in their guts,
dangerous, unexterminable
as 19th century chiaroscuros of saints.

October 18th: I saw one lolloping stray.
It nosed my *simit*, then flopped in the shade
by the ferry to the Asian side, an innocuous
red tag in its lank ear, less fierce by half
than the gargoyle at the Galatasaray —
a stone hound bellowing from its column,
tongue stuck hard and archaic toward the sky.

Catherine Owen

Dusk

Whimpering and willing to be my friend,
she appeared as an apparition at dusk;
we wandered together into a puppified dream.
Yet I was the stray tethered to an invisible leash.
My Alabaster Lady of the Night, my One delight,
bless me with your paws of Solitude and Love
for I have sinned — filling the steamer of my mind
with carnally riven thought sautéed in delicious lust.

Spectre tinted silver as the camera's origins, slipping
behind a dark veil to snap your transience, my plea
is meagre — "benison, benison!" I am only human, after all,
and lack your unclouded bark, the baleful loyalty in your look,
but you lead me on, one paw pressed to the night, beating icon,
soft Mary — you lead me on, and dawn, in its turn, follows.

Joe Rosenblatt & Catherine Owen

A Lost Lover as One of the Ghost-Dogs of Arrum

for Frank

Loping, I can see you, enveloped in the fog's holy
loneliness, a four-legged psychopomp, condemned
to trawl the tidal line between life's sand and death's
raucous ocean. Some have glimpsed you in the headlights,
a fleeting dark stain across the vision. Others tell of beholding you
begging for scraps from absence. Those who took pity fell afoul
of Charon; those who spurned drowned in the River Styx.
It was not your doing.

Your Celtic-boned ancestors were slain for divination, cast
into wells. Who can fault a little ghost-man's revenge? Scavenger-
lover, you who have gored memory, shaken my pith to animal, made
shreds of this rabid obsession to know you, do not scatter my bones in the sun.
Eat me whole and let me enter the underworld. This time we will prowl
diaphanous, your black tongue licking me beyond light's flesh.

Catherine Owen

Canis Minor, the Trojan War's First Muse

Of Orion's glittering pups, he was her favourite
and she, the most ravished spawn of Zeus, his.
Nights when Menelaus was tending to Hermione,
she would stroll inside the palisades with Paris
(erstwhile advisor), star-glommed eyes pressed
to the telescope, taking turns to exclaim the galaxy.
At Orion's belt, their fingers glanced, at his shaft, hips
rubbed, but by Canis Major it was a kiss mashed to lips
caught in awe. Above Monoceros, the impossible,
they eloped, where Canis Minor scoots
a paw toward Ursa's rump. Riding the constellated
seas, knowing only beauty and the twinkling of the moment,
no horse clopped across their passion, glutted with the blood
of a thousand men, only a little bright hound, bearing brightness.

Catherine Owen

Asterion

Little non-entity, looped to Bootes, you
bound ahead of your name — "starry one" —
though affixed to no particular star but
a black cannibal hole in my mind. They
say you have a master, leaner than a comet's tail,
as gentled by riding the light years
from home. Is there home in this gadding universe?
A place to solidly recline and breathe a constellation's

decency? Ursa Major, whom you chase, once
relished the predatorless heavens, she
around since the Ice Age, you a mere pup
of Renaissance avidity. How power
barks your brightness as you strain against time's
leash, amorphous in the northern sky.

Catherine Owen

The Heliacal Rising of Sirius

Who was the brightest nub of corn where the dog ran
Cherokee. Who was the Milky Way's escapee from a sky mill's
mallet. Mutt of the loaf's ontology! Hound from bread's naissance!
It is the convict who leads us to celestial patterns, scatters
a cosmology of intent across the sky's factory-black.
At the apex, you're evidence of crime's divine beauty: embalmer
Anubis, goddess Bau, fierce Hecate; canine-headed Muses,
death's maidenizers. I have wanted you to burn in me

as fired as the dog days of summer, that laborious
love a season melds in the body when motion
is indivisible to tongue-tip on a coal of ice, or paws
ghosting the trawled grass and the mind dreams only
of the Nile, its annual flood filling the lobes with mire,
its relentless swash under the star of thieves.

Catherine Owen

Fluff

I. As Lady of the Manse

Señorita! Languid as summer's first
stoop, pearl-muffed, paws mitred
to rump and stair, sedate as *gracias*
But a poem is no report. You skip
me over the threshold and into the dark
kitchen, the ancient palisades of food
and the upturned face your bowl makes
on the floor, limpid, pure as fish ponds

tended by sad gardeners. The old
noblesse oblige lingers — posing for the lens
of *Turista* like the faint script tradition seeps
into granite. Your body decked out in its fine
linen tablecloth, a butler beneath your lids
beckoning us to so many lost and solemn feasts.

2. As an Apparitional Canine

And why not a harbinger of joy!
The way you spin the light, take
Plato's shadows and twirl with them
in the maw of a Cubano cave to your own
rah-rah. Does delight have a currency?
Fluff is cotton candy, the navel's amnesia.
Fluff catches in the warps and wefts of your hair
as the world dissolves. The poem

proposes to capture, but Fluff rides
a current — *hasta la vista, baby,* to anchors,
chains, the enjambed detente, the conclusive
coup. Fluff shimmies through rhythm's
foliage, lop-life swaying and the sashay haven,
yeah, meets betwixt groin and eye.

Catherine Owen

Flop

Carmen Miranda of the auricular!
In every stray lies a showgirl, silky
circuses the spine plies on street
corners. Coquette, you click your paws
to secretive maracas, swill Anis del Toro,
swoon against your lover's rumbas.
Squatting in the world's siesta, cha cha cha
chimes in that brain, sprung from tamed boulevards.

An epithalamium, your origamied ear be beauty wed
to some bitch tethered by a phantom grin.
That tantalizing ear is like some precious leaf
secured inside a reliquary of ghostly celluloid.
You're Carmen's reincarnation on the prowl for God.
Yes, I'd trade in my mundane ear for your floppy gift!

Joe Rosenblatt & Catherine Owen

The 21st Century: A Letter

Dear readers,
Freud, for once, was bang on: dogs have no shame,
will boink in the busiest thoroughfares, balls a-flap
like flags in the brisk wind of coitus; will drop
steaming plonk on the most eloquently mown lawns;
fart with aplomb and lick, with randy abandon,
the mauve stars of their anuses.
Dog is man's best friend because he shows him

how he once lived and lives still in the rank meadows
of his dreams. But o, *mes semblables*, this dog, it seems,
must die: smothered in its baggie, beaten with Keep
Out signs, buried beneath a muzzle, strangled by a
leash and when Celia grabs my breasts, I shrink,
dear readers,

and the robot puts the dog to sleep.

Catherine Owen

Effigy

Ur-hands once rounded you, pawed from clay
and mire a likeness, of what grave mien? Catfish
whiskered, portentous, stolid as revolution
transfixed by its marching, its long vigil
for justice. You canine tumulus! Carved
hard from your heritage, stuck with aplomb
in the middle of Nothing. I have begged you,
Sphinx-dog, to let me pass, even though

I do not know the answer to what walks
on four legs: morning, siesta, night (its bayed-
at sirens, its steamy humps behind
hydrants). If only, for a moment, I could
be inhuman as you, a million centuries
in your posture, eyes bright as bone-yards, as shameless.

Catherine Owen

"You Old Dog"

in affection — JR/04

With seven years for our every one, seven
digging, scorfing annums in which to take
life by the masseters, each gristly inspiration,
and make it give up its blood,
he slips out of his muzzle like a corset,
snaps his leash's horizon and burns into town,
a whippet riding his mind, to bark his latest
vision at Qualicum's central hydrant.

No doddering his rump by the fire, content
with a scritch between bristly ears and an extra
scrap on Sundays, he's got candles
in his carcanet, a glowing yarmulke, and a ladies'
clip-on in his regal snout; he's his own birthday cake
on four well-trod paws, humping the Muse's dark leg,

tirelessly panting.

Catherine Owen

The Flea Circus of Romance

When a dog-headed man loves a dog-headed woman
together their hearts start tearing around a dog run;
nuzzling snout to snout the wired lovers conjoin —
as paws stick together in those moments of bliss
though they don't imagine that the madness of Tough Love
seethes on Death Row at some seedy city pound,
for when a dog-headed woman loves a dog-headed man
canine delight combusts for that puppified couple.

Lust spins them crazy and sick with heartworm.
No groomer can desnarl their mangled hairy mat;
nor is there a powder for the flea circus of romance
when dog-headed conjoiners disentangle after a romp;
Eros is served up in a dish and often mixed with bile,
for this dog-headed couple delirious with incisors.

Joe Rosenblatt

Behind the Curtain

I am that nocturnal beast snuffling
a curtain of the night to lave
the longitude and latitude of you
and have you moan, weep and writhe to heaven
for you are my vessel of delight.
Let us be a unitary soul and body:
your luminescence and my darkness
on a canvas — au jus, amour — embodied
if you agree — then lay your head upon my urgent paw.
Oh Destiny, throw me a five-inch stiletto black leather shoe.
I am in the kennel now facing the crepuscular dog catcher:
Which dog am I — hand me a leash of burning silver.
And lead me into that dark ether behind the curtain.
Trust in the Dog Star, diadem of a cosmic puppy show.

Joe Rosenblatt

Afterword

When Joe Rosenblatt first saw an exhibition of my *Perros: Dogs of Central Havana* in Vancouver in 2002, he was struck by the mysticism that emanated from the photographs. He saw the Cuban dogs as archetypes, their metaphysics hearkening back to the word's origin in devotional poetry in a metaphorical style relating to God and other sacred entities. Until then, I hadn't conceived of these images as mythopoetic but, thinking back, Joe's reaction doesn't surprise me.

For six weeks in the summer of 2000, I roamed the streets of Havana distressed by the disparity being played out between *turista* and the Cubano. I was a tourist too, but I didn't want to participate in the dance of have and have-nots. I had brought a consciousness regarding issues of injustice with me on my trip to Cuba; I had gone there to experience a country that had had a socialist revolution in the hopes of witnessing an alternative and more just form of society. This naïve idealism had been complicated and compromised by the contradictions I witnessed in Cuban socialism. When I encountered the homeless dogs, skittering on the edges and in the cracks, their constant presence became my courage and my inspiration: they became my spirit guides.

In general, dogs outside of the First World exist as a form of wilderness unique to the societal environment of human poverty they find themselves in. They remain uncomplicated by human fetishization. In the First World, dogs are often luxurious accessories, their owners irrationally devoted to their pets as live consumer products to be dressed up and displayed as an extension of their personalities; outside of the First World, however, the animals are stripped bare to their feral doggedness. Throughout Havana, even the "housed" dogs strut unleashed on their terrain, claiming ownership outside their masters' dwellings while the homeless street dogs, perpetually shifting and outcast, have an aura of survival spirituality that rises out of the half-light of their absent-presence. They live and die in the streets just like homeless people in every kind of society.

Through the poetry of Joe Rosenblatt and Catherine Owen, these *perros* of Havana have formally moved from the streets of the real to the real of mythology. Their courage, survival, suffering and joy have transcended the realities of the flesh and become sublime. Chiseled, hammered now into the stone of poetry, these dogs that guided me through *a bite of life* have gradually shed their vulnerability and become the ferocity of myth: *stone hounds bellowing* essences of dog. And *our spirits follow, puppified.*

Karen Moe
January 2008

About The Authors

Karen Moe is a photographer and multi-media performance artist. Her work has been published in *West Coast Line, dandelion, Prairie Fire* and *subterrain*. She recently collaborated with Catherine Owen in *Cusp/detritus: an Experiment in Alleyways* which was published by Anvil Press in 2006. The detritus pieces were exhibited in Vancouver at Exposure Gallery in 2005 and The Whip Gallery in 2006. *Lethe: a mock metaphysics* was performed and exhibited at Xchanges Gallery in Victoria. *Perros: Dogs of Central Havana* were exhibited at the Havana Gallery in Vancouver in 2002 and Pteros Gallery in Toronto in 2005 in participation with The Contact Photography Festival. She is currently completing her latest photographic project, *Sea Surfaces.*

Catherine Owen has been publishing and performing poetry since 1993. Her work has appeared in periodicals such as *The Dalhousie Review* and *Poetry Salzburg*. Titles include *Somatic – The Life and Work of Egon Schiele* (Exile Editions 1998), nominated for the Gerald Lampert Award; *The Wrecks of Eden* (Wolsak and Wynn, 2002), shortlisted for the B.C. Book Prize; and her new collections, *Shall: ghazals* (Wolsak and Wynn, 2006) and *Cusp/detritus* (Anvil Press, 2006), both long-listed for the Relit Prize, while the latter made the shortlist for the George Ryga Award for socially conscious literature. A selection from *Seeing Lessons*, on the pioneer photographer Mattie Gunterman, was recently nominated for the CBC Literary Awards. Her poems have been translated into Italian and Korean. She has a Masters degree in English (Simon Fraser University, 2001), collaborates with painters/dancers, practices photography and plays bass/sings in the eco-metal band INHUMAN.

Joe Rosenblatt was born in Toronto in 1933. He dropped out of trade school as a young adult and worked at a series of low-paying jobs until he started working as a labourer for the Canadian Pacific Railway in 1956. He became interested in writing through his association with the worker poet Milton Acorn in the early '60s and the metaphysical poetry of Gwendolyn MacEwen. By 1966 he had his first book of poetry published and he also received a Canada Council grant that allowed him to leave his job as a freight handler on the old Canadian Pacific Railway and devote the next year to writing and travelling. Over the years, Rosenblatt has written more than 20 books of poetry and several autobiographical works, and his poems have appeared in over 30 anthologies of Canadian poetry over his 40-year career as a poet. His poetry books have received major awards, such as the Governor General's Award for poetry in 1976 and the B.C. Book Prize in 1986. He has travelled widely, giving readings of his poems in Europe, Canada and the United States. Several bilingual volumes of his poetry have been published in Italian with translations by the late Prof. Alfredo Rizzardi of the University of Bologna, and Ada Donati of Rome. His poems have also been translated into French, Dutch, Swedish and Spanish. For the past 27 years, Rosenblatt has been living in the resort community of Qualicum Beach on Vancouver Island with his wife Faye and their three cats.

Acknowledgements

A selection of these dog sonnets were originally published as *Caneide* (trans. Ada Donati; Fasono di Brindisi, Italy: Schena Editore, 2005).

Others have appeared in the journals Exile: The Literary Quarterly, The Malahat Review, Prairie Fire, and The Dalhousie Review, as well as the anthology *Jailbreaks: 99 Canadian Sonnets* (ed. Zachariah Wells; Biblioasis, 2008).